END

Evon Horton has written an insightful and inspiring book. *Spiritual Seasons* will give you a fresh perspective on your moment of life. He tells readers that although you cannot rush a seasonal change, you can trace the hand of God.

TED TRAYLOR
Olive Baptist Church
Pensacola, Florida

Dr. Evon Horton is a pastor to pastors. For over a decade, I have been able to watch him skillfully lead Brownsville Assembly through both difficult and fruitful seasons. In his book, *Spiritual Seasons*, Dr. Evon uses life and ministry lessons to teach us to make the most of the seasons we are in.

AARON BURKE
Lead Pastor, Radiant Church
Tampa, Florida

My heart is so stirred by the powerful new book, *Spiritual Seasons,* written by my friend Dr. Evon Horton! This book is a must-read for everyone in search of knowing their "Kiros" season as a Christian and leader. One of the greatest mysteries we all face in life is knowing what season that we are in. It will bring revelation to your present situation and launch you into your destiny. I have often said, "The calling of God, without the timing of God, will result in the absence of God." We must realize our present season. This book will explain the quiet, mundane and loud seasons of life. It is a map for a journey to the center of God's plan for you. GET THIS BOOK!"

Pat Schatzline
Evangelist and author
Remnant Ministries International

SPIRITUAL SEASONS

ANOTHER BOOK BY EVON HORTON

From a Father's Heart

SPIRITUAL SEASONS

DISCERNING AND FLOURISHING IN EVERY SEASON OF LIFE

EVON HORTON

DESTINY IMAGE® PUBLISHERS, INC.
PO Box 310, Shippensburg, PA 17257-0310
"Promoting Inspired Lives."

This book and all other Destiny Image and Destiny Image Fiction books are available at Christian bookstores and distributors worldwide.

Cover design by Eileen Rockwell
Interior design by Terry Clifton

For more information on foreign distributors, call 717-532-3040.
Or reach us on the Internet: www.destinyimage.com

ISBN 13 TP: 978-0-7684-4619-7
ISBN 13 EBook: 978-0-7684-4620-3
ISBN LP: 978-0-7684-4621-0
ISBN HC: 978-0-7684-4622-7

For Worldwide Distribution, Printed in the U.S.A.

1 2 3 4 5 6 / 21 20 19 18

ACKNOWLEDGMENTS

I would like to acknowledge the following:

- Larry Sparks from *Destiny Image* for encouraging me to get this message published
- Marilyn Hickey, who has amazed me with her practical application of Scripture and for writing the gracious forward for this book
- Claude Horton, my father
- Robert Taitinger, former General Superintendent of the Assemblies in Canada
- Bob Smith, who mentored me as a newly Spirit-filled pastor
- Ken Birch, who took a risk and hired me as his associate at MGT

DEDICATION

I'd like to dedicate this book to my four Grandchildren, Charlotte, Ethan, William and a new one coming in a few months. Being a grandfather has underscored the reality and truth of Spiritual Seasons!

There is a time for everything
and a season for every activity
under the heavens.
—ECCLESIASTES 3:1

CONTENTS

FOREWORD

Pastor Evon Horton has a true pastor's heart! Certainly when he writes, he writes from his knowledge but also his life experiences as a pastor. I believe there is much wisdom in this book; and as it helps those of us who have pastored, it will also help others. I have known Pastor Evon a long time and appreciate him as a man of prayer. Many times he has called and shared his faith with me for my prayer needs.

What you will receive out of this book lines up with Ecclesiastes 3:11, *"He has made everything beautiful in its time."* As you read this book, you will realize whatever season you are in, God will make it beautiful!

MARILYN HICKEY
Founder, Marilyn Hickey Ministries
Best-selling Author
International Evangelist

INTRODUCTION

As long as the earth endures, seedtime and harvest, cold and heat, summer and winter, day and night will never cease.

—Genesis 8:22

God created seasons. They are part of the DNA of planet Earth. These seasons occur on a regular basis, not just in nature but also in our lives.

Our journey in life and our relationships, with Him and others, all revolve around *spiritual seasons.*

In this book, we'll journey through these seasons. We will understand that seasons come and seasons go. We will see how our lives change as we go through them. We will discover that the seasons of life touch our occupations, studies, and relationships with family and God.

Be open in spirit, mind, and soul as you read through this book. Let the Holy Spirit speak to you to discern and understand what spiritual season you are in currently.

Then discover how to respond to that season with all its possibilities and fullness. The Lord is definitely guiding your footsteps and wants you to be fulfilled in all His goodness, plan, and provision for your life!

1

SEASONS—GOD'S CREATIONS

There is a time for everything
and a season for every activity
under the heavens.
—Ecclesiastes 3:1

There are seasons in nature, but also in life. Perhaps my favorite season is the Christmas season! I love the anticipation, the gift giving, the gift receiving. The gathering of family is also very important. All of the special foods and traditions make the Christmas season wondrous. I love the tradition of Santa Claus. Someone once said there are four seasons of a man as he relates to Santa Claus. The first season, as a child, believes in Santa. The second, he does not believe! The third, he is Santa Claus. And last, he looks like Santa!

Spiritual Seasons of a Believer

The same is true when it comes to the seasons of a believer in Christ, a Christian. There are definitely four distinct seasons of a Christian:

Season One

The first season, *crawling:* babes learning what it is to follow Jesus. They are inquisitive and trusting. That first season, baby Christians are so excited, and yet so naïve.

Season Two

The second season is *walking:* learning how to stand on our own two feet. The second season is testing out our spiritual legs. I remember when our children were learning to walk and stumbling and falling and bumping into things. We were so excited when they started walking. I recall thinking to myself, when they were getting into everything and disappearing from room to room, toddling their way around the house, *Why did I ever encourage this walking thing?*

This is when you are taking steps on your own, memorizing Scriptures, and learning the power of prayer. Even learning how to run with God's vision and plan for your life. That second season is so powerful, so fresh, so new, so bright. I remember clearly discovering God's Word and promises and getting so excited that God's Word is true today. Wow! Powerful times.

I spoke to someone recently who had great impact on my life when I was younger. His name is Wayne Watson and is a retired school teacher. He was a phenomenal musician and could play the piano like I had never seen or heard before. I remember being at the campground of my childhood, standing next to the old upright piano in the tabernacle, watching his fingers fly on the ivories of that old piano. When I spoke to him, he commented how he had watched me grow up and become a minister with such passion and zeal. Now at this stage of my ministry when I am transitioning to teaching and mentoring, I want to be an encouragement to young people like Wayne was to me. I want to help them discover their potential in Christ. I want to tell them to run with all they have for God and that God will bless them in their incredible season.

Season Three

That brings me to the third season of believers. This is a season of *sitting*. The first season we crawl, the second season we walk and run, now we sit. The traditional position of a teacher is sitting. Jesus is quite often referred to in Scripture as Raboni, Rabbi, and Teacher. The Bible says in the Gospel of John chapter 8 verse 2:

> *At dawn he [Jesus] appeared again in the temple courts, where all the people gathered around him, and he sat down to teach them.*

This third season comes as you sit and share your stories—the lessons you've learned on your journey through life. Stories that may have been passed down through the ages. This is a powerful time. Where your stories are your stories and no one can take away from your stories.

I remember clearly sharing hundreds of times my testimony of spiritual renewal. I shared when and where my wife, Deborah, and I were filled with the power of the Holy Spirit. It was a true Acts 2 experience. It was the fulfillment of Acts 1:8 (NKJV), *"But you shall receive power when the Holy Spirit has come upon you...."* This is my story, and no one can tell me it's wrong. I simply share this is what happened to me and no one argue with that!

THERE ARE MOMENTS IN LIFE WHEN YOU NEED TO TAKE A STAND.

The third season is where you can pass on what you have learned in life. It's a time of investing in others. It's a mature time in life when you share with others so they can avoid the mistakes you've made along the way.

There are moments in life when you need to take a stand. I clearly remember several times in life when my faith, my convictions, my life commitment was being challenged. And I knew that I had to take a stand. It's tough. I am not one to be argumentative or confrontational. But I do know there are moments when we get called into account.

I need to say—no, this is what I believe. I remember standing with a young man new to ministry. His name is Trey Myers. Trey was miraculously delivered from drugs and left his trade of dealing drugs. It was a dramatic conversion. Trey was one who pushed the envelope to seek more of God and His life-changing power. He would say some outlandish things that made people raise their eyebrows, too. He said once that he had seen Jesus physically appear before him. Someone came to me who had heard Trey say that and the person told me that it was hard to believe and Trey was crazy. I knew I had to take a stand and support this young man. I knew it may have sounded crazy to some, but I took a stand. I believe and know that Trey did see Jesus. I believe it.

Season Four

The final season, the fourth, is *standing*. You're not crawling, you're not walking or running, and you're not sitting teaching. This is a season where you know when to stand and hold firm. This is a season when you know what you believe and are willing to stand up for it—even unto death.

Seasons of Challenge

It has taken me a long time to appreciate the four seasons of my Christian life. In fact, if I'm totally honest, I still struggle with some of the seasons that God has me go through. There have been tough struggles, tough days. My current assignment at Brownsville Assembly of God in Pensacola, Florida, has been the most challenging season of my ministry.

When I arrived, the church was in post revival. The season of Revival at Brownsville Assembly (1995-2000) was real, genuine, chaotic, monumental, life-changing, and difficult. My calling to Brownsville was to help this church recover from a season as a revival center to that of a healthy local church. But I still wanted the power of the Holy Spirit and revival to stay in the church—and it has.

I found myself in a church that was in free fall. The facility was worn and needed much TLC. The congregation had declined to less than 500. And the cumulative debt for the church and ministry school was over $10 million. The monthly mortgage payment was $83,000. Ouch! Talk about a tough season.

But the one thing I knew was God had called me to pastor this church, this congregation, this church family through this difficult season.

Someone asked me once if I was enjoying my season at Brownsville. I'm not sure if that was the right question. Enjoyment was not the word I would have used at that time. Did I know I was called to Brownsville? YES! Was I fulfilled in being in the center of the Lord's will? YES! Was it enjoyable? Not always!

SEASONS ARE EXPERIENCED IN NATURE, RELATIONSHIPS, CAREERS, MINISTRY, AND EVEN IN CHURCHES.

What this season at Brownsville has taught me is that there are seasons in ministry, in life, and in churches. And our role as Christians is to discover what season we are in and what role God has called us to play.

Another realization is that I can't force the season to change. I can argue that I don't like the season; I can complain about how hard the season is. But I know I can't change the season. Seasons are a God thing. Seasons are God's creation and doing.

In the next chapter I share with you some lessons I've learned about the seasons in life.

2

FIVE LESSONS ABOUT SEASONS

The following are five lessons I've learned about spiritual seasons during my lifetime. I share these to help you understand how much—or how little—control you have over the seasons in your life.

1. The season you are in currently is controlled by God.

2. Seasons of life are sometimes misunderstood.

3. God doesn't do anything by accident.

4. The seasons of your life will include good and bad, easy and difficult, ups and downs.

5. There are four seasons in each relationship.

Let's examine each of these five lessons more closely.

1. The season you are in currently is controlled by God.

Daniel 2:21 says that God, *"changes times and seasons."* The Good News translation says it this way, God *"controls the times and the seasons."* God is in control of the seasons of your life. You can't force one season to close and another to start. Just like you can't stop winter or start springtime. Each season arrives and departs in God's timing—in due season!

2. Seasons of life are sometimes misunderstood.

The seasons of life are confusing. It's hard to understand when all of a sudden God takes us into a new season. We struggle with the transition and question His motives.

In the New Century Version Ecclesiastes 3:11 says, *"He [God] does everything just right and on time, but people can never completely understand what he is doing."* We need to realize the Christian life is lived by faith—not by explanation. We quite often want God to explain everything He's doing. And He rarely does.

We do need to rest assured that He has a purpose for each season. The Living Bible says, *"We know that all that happens to us is working for our good if we love God and are fitting into his plans"* (Romans 8:28).

I clearly recall when I felt it was time for me to close my time as president of Master's College and Seminary in Ontario, Canada. The Pentecostal Assemblies of Canada leadership had asked me to implement a new model of ministry training. It had been approved by all the districts supporting the school with overwhelming majorities, most of them in the 90th percentile.

However, when I actually began implementation, we hit tremendous resistance. It was a tough five years of leadership. But now I felt my season was over and it was time to move on. That fall I found that Grand Rapids First Assembly church was looking for a senior pastor. Wayne Benson, former senior pastor, had my name placed on the list of candidates. I received a call from the chair of the pastoral search committee. He was a fine man, lawyer by trade. We dialogued through the process, and he asked about me, my call, gifts, etc. During the journey, I found myself helping him with the pastoral search process. What the next steps were, etc.

Deborah and I traveled to Grand Rapids and met with the search committee and had a wonderful time. I truly felt this position was a match made in Heaven! Grand Rapids was Deborah's hometown and her parents retired just north of the city. It was truly a God thing!

The chair of the search committee shared with me that they had narrowed the field to three candidates, and I was one of them. I thought, *God is confirming our call to Grand Rapids!*

A couple of weeks following the narrowing of the field I received a call informing me that the committee had chosen one of the other candidates. What was difficult was the chairperson remarked that he couldn't have done his job as well as he did if he weren't for my guiding him through the process, and he wanted to sincerely thank me!

I was confused and didn't understand. It was a hard season for me. I didn't accept the disappointment well. I felt God had forgotten me. It was now December and winter was in full swing in Toronto—and in my own life.

I remember clearly the day when I received the call in January, the next month, from Dr. Mark Rutland, president of Southeastern University in Lakeland, Florida. His words still ring in my memory. He said, "Evon, I want you to come here and be the Dean of the School of Ministry training at Southeastern. I need you to revamp it like you did Master's. Come and do what you did there! There is no short list...you are it! The only question is, what will it take to get you here!" WOW! I was overwhelmed. It was a new season. *I'm going to Lakeland to help a university redevelop its mission and mandate to train ministers for the future!*

Deborah and I flew to Florida in February and met with Dr. Rutland, the academic VP, HR, and others. It was set. We were going to Lakeland. Our daughter and new son-in-law were living in Winter Haven, just a few miles outside of Lakeland. We found a home a few blocks from them and the owners accepted our offer to purchase. God had it all under control. We flew back to Canada, ready to make the move. I told the Board of Governors of Master's College and Seminary that I was resigning and we were moving to Florida.

Then the first week of March, I received a call from Dr. Rutland and he said he just got off a long plane ride to Alaska and the Lord told him while on the flight that I was not the one, and he needed to rescind the offer of a position. *WHAT?! Lord, what are you doing to me? I'm stuck in this winter season. I don't understand what You're doing.*

Graduation was in April for Master's, followed by Board of Governor's meetings. During a Board of Governor's meeting, my cell phone rang—it was Mark Rutland. As I see his name on the phone screen, I'm thinking, *There's no way I'm going to take this call.* But I did.

Mark told me he had just preached at a church that needed a pastor, and he recommended me. In fact, he said, "There's only one person I think could handle this job and it's you." I'm thinking, *Yeah, right!*

He told me that the chair of the search committee would be calling me—with an 850 area code phone number—and he encourage me to take the call. Sure enough, about ten minutes later I received a call from David Mayo, the chair of the search committee for Brownsville Assembly in Pensacola, Florida. Brownsville was the home to the largest and longest running revival in U.S. history. Five million people attended over six years. Even though I had never attended, I was very familiar with the revival.

Wayne Benson, former senior pastor of Grand Rapids First Assembly was healed at the revival in Brownsville, and then revival broke out in Grand Rapids. He actually had the team from Brownsville come to Michigan to hold an Awake America crusade. I took our whole pastoral team from Mississauga to attend. It was powerful.

As I chatted with David, we made arrangements for Deborah and I to visit the last weekend of June. It was an amazing time, and God's call was evident. At the writing of this book, we are finishing our twelfth year here as senior pastors. And the winter season was over.

That brings me to the next point. God doesn't do anything by accident. The two false starts from Grand Rapids and Southeastern prepared me for the call to Pensacola. The Southeastern connection with Mark allowed him to get to know my gifts, my strengths, weaknesses, and me. He realized I was the one the Lord was calling to meet this difficult need for the church in Pensacola.

3. *God doesn't do anything by accident.*

The season you're in currently isn't a surprise to God. He can use every aspect of it for your good!

I was extremely frustrated through that last season and didn't know what God was doing. I even questioned if He'd forgotten me. I started looking for teaching positions and even jobs at Disney. I was lost. But I really wasn't lost. The Lord knew exactly where I was and what I needed, and when I needed it!

4. *The seasons of your life will include good and bad, easy and difficult, ups and downs.*

When you read through Ecclesiastes 3:2-8 you see a long list of times of things that occur. Both positive and negative occur in our lives, both good and bad, both designating ups and downs.

> *There is a time for everything, and a season for every activity under the heavens: a time to be born and a time to die, a time to plant and a time to uproot, a time to kill and a time to heal, a time*

> *to tear down and a time to build, a time to weep and a time to laugh, a time to mourn and a time to dance, a time to scatter stones and a time to gather them, a time to embrace and a time to refrain from embracing, a time to search and a time to give up, a time to keep and a time to throw away, a time to tear and a time to mend, a time to be silent and a time to speak, a time to love and a time to hate, a time for war and a time for peace* (Ecclesiastes 3:1-8).

I want to be completely transparent. I can't stand the tough seasons, the difficult seasons, the valley experiences. But I also realize that going through those seasons and experiences is when I learn the most. I love the mountaintop experiences. I love the spring season with new life, the summer season filled with lazy days, and the fall when the harvest is abundant and plentiful. But I don't like the winters. When things are hard. When things are difficult.

A few weeks ago, I met with the Florida Governor Rick Scott. His term limit is up next year and he's running for U.S. Senate. I received a call from his office saying he was coming to Pensacola and wanted to meet with pastors and invited me to come. I said yes. The caller asked if I knew of anyone else who could or should be invited to attend. I asked if Joey Rogers, pastor at Pace Assembly, was on the list. The caller said no but I could invite him. I reached out to Joey and he also attended.

On the day of the meeting when I arrived at Olive Baptist church, I realized the only pastors there were Ted Traylor, Olive Baptist pastor, Joey, and me. There were some others from Olive there, but the only pastors were the three of us. Wow! Pretty humbling to have an hour and a half with the governor of Florida to hear our concerns for the city, state, and country.

In dialoguing with Governor Scott, he asked us if ministry was as hard as being governor—that everything he does seems to be met with resistance. Even if in his mind something is good and not a difficult decision, it ends up being a struggle. We told him that ministry in the church is no different. It's always a battle.

So it is in seeing the seasons of life. There are all four!

Before leaving, the Governor asked if we had any other questions. I said yes and asked, "Because you are seeking election as a U.S. Senator, what do I say to the people of Brownsville, an impoverished, struggling community, when they ask me why they should vote for you." He quickly responded without hesitation, "Ask me to come to Brownsville and I'll tell them." I told him to consider himself invited. I've had two or three subsequent conversations with the Governor's team, and we are currently working on a date for him to come to Brownsville. But the details of that visit will have to be in another book.

I was surprised to be included in this group; I was surprised to meet the Governor; I was surprised he offered to come and visit Brownsville. God is full of surprises.

The church is currently going through another difficult time financially. But I realize this season is not a surprise to God and He has a plan to see us through it. Through each season I remember the Word says:

There is a time to:

live/die...

plant/uproot...

gather/scatter...

keep/throw away...

repair/tear...

speak up/be quiet...

find/lose...

build/tear down...

heal/kill...

laugh/cry...

peace/war...

love/hate...

dance/grieve...

With the opposites of variance in what occurs in each of the seasons, you can realize that what you learn in one season, you'll use in another. Isn't that what happens with the farmer and the seasons of the fields on the farm? What he sows in one season, he is able to reap a harvest in another. Paul commended these words to the church in Galatia in Galatians 6:9 (NKJV), *"Let us not grow weary while doing good, for in due season we shall reap if we do not lose heart."*

A friend of mine in Canada, Gary Empey, talked about being in ministry this way. He said as a minister you have the fruit of the Spirit growing in your life. You have love growing, also joy, peace, patience, kindness, goodness, faithfulness, gentleness, and self-control. These are attributes of the fruit of God growing in your life. But in ministry those you minister too come along and pick your fruit. They take some of your peace, they pick your patience, and test your self-control. After a while, all the fruit you are currently bearing in your life is picked. You are fruit tree that has been "picked clean"! You have no fruit left.

When this becomes evident, you need to get away and give yourself time to grow some more fruit. The fall season of harvest is over. Now it's time to grow some more fruit in your life.

Another analogy came from one of the many I've had on staff as a youth pastor. Eldon Wright was one of the best! He said youth ministry or just ministry in general is like surfing. You get on your surfboard, paddle out into the surf, pushing through incoming waves crashing over you and your board. You eventually get out far enough to see the big wave coming. At just the right time, you jump up on your board and ride the wave to shore. When you hit the shore, you're exhausted and flake out on the beach trying to catch your breath. Once you've recovered, you grab your surf board and start paddling out again to catch another big wave.

I guess to say all that is to say, the seasons of life, ministry, relationships, etc. are all the same. You push, you struggle, you ride it out, and then you recover. There are seasons.

Questions to Consider

Before moving to the specifics of the four different seasons, let's consider some evaluative questions about the season you're in currently based on what you've read so far.

- How would you describe the current season?
- What does it feel like, winter, spring, summer, or fall?
- Once you've determined which season you're in, ask yourself, *What is the right response for this season?*

A farmer knows the right response for the particular season approaching. In the spring, he prepares the field and plants the seed. In the summer, he fertilizes, weeds, and waters. In the fall he harvests the crops. The winter is a time of rest and planning for the next season. We need to have the right work ethic for every time of life. The wrong response on our part can destroy God's perfect plan for us.

Know your season. Determine your plan of action to be successful.

5. There are four seasons in each relationship.

Spring. Spring is when you start a relationship and you begin to invest in it. Maybe you even give more than you're getting out of it because you can sense possibilities. You want to invest and plant even though you don't see any real benefit at the start. You begin a commitment.

Deborah and I were 19 years of age when we started dating and I eventually proposed marriage. It was a wonderful season. So exciting. So new to both of us to be in love—this is the spring season of a relationship. We were 20 years of age when we were married. Just kids! But thankfully God took pity on us and led us through the spring season of our relationship.

Summer is when the relationship is growing. You see obvious and visible sprouting of communication in common goals and values.

Deborah's and my summer season was wonderful. We loved pastoring; we loved discovering new places together. We loved setting up our homes and doing ministry together. As we grew in our marriage, we grew in our family, and we grew in ministry together. It was a wonderful summer season.

Fall is when you receive benefits from the relationship. The benefit is not just visible, now it's tangible. When you care about someone and he or she cares about you, you are able to see fruit from that relationship.

The fall season for Deborah and ne is our relationship with our grandchildren. Deborah has said many times to me, "I thought when we had children that they would grow up and get married." What we didn't see ahead was the fall season of the harvest of our lives—our grandchildren. Amazing. We love our family so much. We see our grandchildren growing now and coming into their own as little persons. We love them so much. We are so proud of our two daughters and sons-in-law. They are doing amazing things for the Lord and their families. They are truly making a difference.

Winter is the hard season. No one likes to talk about that one. The winter season in a relationship is when you sense the coming of death. It's a time of coldness. The commitment has faded. The relationship seems suspended in animation and frozen in time. It's just plain hard. At those times, you have to realize that a spring thaw can come.

A relationship can be revitalized, but it's hard work. It's so much easier to keep it alive in the first place than to bring it back from the dead.

The winter season for Deborah and I hasn't come. But we have had some people close to us lose their spouse. It's so hard to see someone who was married and loved their spouse for 40-plus years and then death came knocking. It's little comfort to say, "Yes they are in Heaven. But we are left here." I don't honestly know how I would react if I lost Deborah. She's the love of my life.

David Padgett is on staff at Brownsville and he's in charge of the church facilities. But he's more than a staff member. He's become a friend, a brother. He lost his wife to a two-year battle with cancer. They were married 37 years. It's been almost a year since her passing, and I can still see the winter season of grief in his eyes. It's horrible. Again, I don't understand it, I don't like it. I tell David frequently, "I can't imagine what you're going through." It's pretty tough.

3

COMMITMENTS IN LIFE

Commitment to Your Marriage

Spring: planting, investing and starting your marriage together

Summer: growing, sprouting up

Fall: harvesting, when you are needing to receive something tangible out of the time together

Winter: hard times, cold, no response, tough

Commitment to Your Children

Spring: investing in your children when they are young

Summer: watching them grow and enjoying their soccer games, recitals, etc.

Fall: harvesting, at some time you receive a harvest and a blessing from them

Winter: hard times, cold, no response, tough, no communication

Emily, our youngest, went through a tough time. She met a young man at Southeastern, fell in love, got married, and had a child. He wanted to be a doctor; he wanted to go into ministry. So many dreams and spring aspirations.

Then they started drifting away from us, the church, and the Lord. I remember praying for her over and over again. I told her three things during that winter season. I love you, I care about you, I'm praying for you!

What I didn't know was her husband was caught up in drugs and the relationship had turned violent and physically abusive. I'll never forget one late Sunday night, Deborah and I were going to bed and my phone rang. It was Emily. "Can you come and pick up William and me?" I said, "I'll be right there." She stayed with us. Went through recovery counseling. She is now married to a wonderful husband who is a wonderful dad to her son.

But boy, that winter season, wondering if she'd ever come home, was awful and horrible.

The story in the Bible that I use to give others comfort during these types of circumstances is the story of the prodigal son. In Luke 15:20 it says, *"But while he was still a long way off, his father saw him and was filled with compassion for him; he ran to his son, threw his arms around him...."* That is what God does for those waiting for the return of a loved one. He is waiting just like we are. And even though our loved one may be a long way off, our heavenly

Father is waiting and sees and runs and throws His arms around us. He is with us through the waiting.

Commitment to Your Job

> *Spring:* planting, investing and starting, working hard, going beyond the expected
>
> *Summer:* growing, sprouting up, rising through the ranks, enjoying the promotions
>
> *Fall:* harvesting, when you need to receive something tangible, the vacations, the bonus
>
> *Winter:* hard times, cold, tough, but you hang in throughout this season, the pink slip, downsizing, job loss

We all enter new employment opportunities believing it will be an awesome, successful venture. However, we eventually realize there are seasons during our employment years. We have ups and downs. Good and bad experiences. We need to take all four seasons' characteristics into account while working.

Commitment to Your Church

Spring: planting, investing and starting in a church, volunteer, donate time, donate money

Summer: growing, sprouting up, as you mature in your relationship with Christ, expansion, building progress, debt reduction

Fall: harvesting, to be on the receiving end of the fellowship

Winter: hard times, cold, no response, tough, the church is going through a tough time

Many won't stand with a church in the winter season. Too many won't stay through difficult times. The easiest solution is to leave.

As a pastor, I particularly have something to say about people's commitment to their church. Too often I hear people say, "The Lord has released me from the church and I'm going elsewhere." I clearly remember Harold Percy, a good friend and Anglican priest of a church in Canada near where I pastored, say, "When someone tells you God is leading them elsewhere. That's Greek for, 'I've found someone who preaches better than you.'" I truly believe God has seasons in churches as well. A church will go through seasons. Ups and downs. Tough times and blessed times. I truly believe just as the Lord gives relationships seasons and individuals seasons, there are seasons in a church as well.

Perhaps one of the most difficult messages I've had to communicate to the church here at Brownsville is as wonderful as the season of the revival was for this church, that season is over. I sense the Lord's presence strongly; we have wonderful services, but the season of night after night services until 1:00 or 2:00 in the morning is over. Now I'm not saying it won't happen again, but I am saying that season is over and I'm going to identify and walk in the season that God currently has for this wonderful church.

Commitment to God

Spring: planting, make a commitment, study and learn all you can, investing and starting your relationship with God, everything is new and you're young in Christ—a newborn baby as the Bible says

Summer: the relationship grows, learning is a joy, spending time together is a pleasure

Fall: harvesting, the investment pays, when trouble comes He sustains and supports when you need to receive something tangible out of the time together; this is a time when you need to receive something from Him while you're going through a hard time

Winter: hard times, cold, no response, tough; many people find this difficult. They feel the Lord has abandoned them. They don't understand why they

> can't feel Him or see God working in their lives. The relationship has grown cold. Many times there is nothing at all wrong. But God has gone silent, and you can't find Him. Realize it's only for a season and He will break through the frozen cold that seems to have formed over your relationship. Reevaluate the commitment.

While pastoring in Mississauga in Canada, there was a wonderful lady in the church whose husband worked at the Assemblies National office. The first time she came to see me, she asked if I could tell if she was saved and going to Heaven. I asked her if she'd received the Lord as her Savior and she assured me that happened many years ago and that she still loved the Lord with all her heart. Based on what she said, then yes she was saved and going to Heaven. She then asked me why she didn't feel as though she were saved.

That conversation began a two-year journey with her periodically coming to my office for prayer, to the altar following service for prayer, or a voicemail or note saying she was still having a difficult time. I don't fully understand why, but for two years she was in a winter season in her relationship with God. Her prayers "bounced off the ceiling," as she put it. She did not have any assurance whatsoever that she was saved and had the Lord's saving grace in her life.

I felt horrible for her. I couldn't help but think of Job, and how he lost it all though he didn't deserve to lose it all and perhaps questioned God immensely. A tough season and a tough place to be. But God got her through this season. She told me it happened one cold winter morning, with snow on the kitchen windowsill. She looked out and saw a little bird hop right on the ledge of the window. She said she realized that God had created this little bird, and cared for it. And if He cared for it, He cared for her. All of a sudden that realization permeated the cold ground of her soul and she was filled with the warmth and presence of God.

Wow! I don't fully understand all of that and why the Lord took her through that season, but I have since that time walked with several who have felt the hand of God lift from their lives for a season, and they struggle.

And to be completely transparent, there have been times when I felt I was struggling with the lack of the presence of the Lord in my life. I knew in my mind that my relationship and call were solid, but the coldness of my heart and relationship was a struggle, and I needed the Lord to melt the frozen sense in my heart with His presence and Spirit.

God's Commitment to You

Here's an interesting one—God's seasons with you!

> *Spring:* planting, investing in you, God makes a deposit of seeds inside you
>
> *Summer:* growing, sprouting up, God sees the seedlings start to sprout up and grow
>
> *Fall:* harvesting, times when He harvests from your life what is needed for

the next step in your relationship with Him

Winter: hard times, cold, no response, tough; a season when we grow cold and can't respond; but it's only a season and there will be a thaw where you can break through

Four Steps in Understanding Your Season

1. Realize

Realize and try to understand that you might be changing from one season to another. All seasons are different. All will pass eventually. This realization is easier said than done. I want God to deliver me from some of the circumstances of a season, but I have to walk it out. And trust He will get me through it. That is the reality—the only way to get to the next season is to walk through the current one. I may want to skip seasons, and quite often the current season I am in. I may want God to supernaturally transport me to the next one, but that doesn't happen. I have to walk it out! You have to walk it out too. Trust in Him!

2. Discover

Be honest with yourself and ask yourself tough questions. What does it feel like, what do you see, what is going on around you? Start to evaluate your current circumstances in order to discover what season you are in now. Too often we play spiritual games with ourselves, saying we are okay, when we're not. We're not honest with our current feelings and emotions and struggles. I pray the Lord will help you, as He does me, to get us to the place where we trust Him in *all seasons!* John Eldridge says in his book *Wild at Heart*, "God will take you on an incredible adventure. During that adventure you'll discover wonderful and phenomenal ways God will be working in your life."

3. Embrace

Embrace the season. People in all different climates and geographies have learned how to embrace the seasons that surround them. In the north during winter, go sledding. In the south in the summer when it's hot, go swimming. In the fall, take a hike in the woods and enjoy the beauty and color. Embrace whatever season you are in. Don't wish time away. Embrace each season as it unfolds and learn something new. There is purpose where you are today!

The seasons have ups and downs, good and bad. We need to see what we can benefit from in those different times. When we relax, take a deep breath, and trust Him, I believe the Lord can get us through whatever season we are facing. Again, this is easier said than done! Embracing the current season with honesty and integrity of heart and spirit is the key. Saying, "Lord, I trust You and I know You only want what's best for me. So I embrace this current season."

4. Celebrate

You will always do better when you are able to celebrate and say truly to God, "Thank You for the season I am in; I want to fulfill all that is possible for my journey in this season." Admittedly, that too is easier said than done! I don't always like the season I'm in. But I can truly say, "Lord, help me celebrate this season, let me learn what I need to learn, and let me find the joy in the season I'm in." Open your mind, open your heart, open your spirit to Him! God really does have only your best interest at heart.

One thing I have always said in ministry, family, marriage, and with friends—the journey is as important as the destination. We want to get there, but how we get there is just as significant.

THE JOURNEY IS AS IMPORTANT AS THE DESTINATION.

One of the reasons I married Deborah was for that very reason. My goal when we were dating and going on day date trips was to get to our destination as fast as possible. I'd drive by a cute store or shop and she'd say, "Can we stop?" I would always say, "Nope, sorry, already passed by." Eventually, after numerous hurried trips, she'd say, "Let's turn around and go back." No way! I didn't want to do that. Slowly, I discovered that the journey could be as much fun as reaching the destination.

Now I realize that God wants to work in my life all along the way. All along life's journey, He wants to process me, purify my heart and life. And He wants to do the same for you.

I remember Chuck and Bev Frankish. They were not only parishioners and I was their pastor, but they became good friends, too. During Chuck's residency, the two of us became spiritual accountability partners. He walked into my life a couple of times.

One time when we met, he asked how I was doing. I told him flippantly, "I wish there were eight days in the week!" He asked why. I said, "Then I could get done all that I needed to do." He told me that the Lord has given me all the time I needed to accomplish His will, and if I don't have enough time, then something on my list isn't in His will and I'm OUT of the Lord's will! OUCH! That hurt to hear—but Chuck was right. I needed to rethink what I was doing.

Another time we met, I remember telling him my priority in life was to get my list completed. I was a list maker, and the best feeling was completing the list. Chuck said that if that's my goal and all that's important is getting the list done, then the ultimate goal is to get life over with.

Wow. I had never thought of it that way. I realized then that the journey was as important as the destination. I pray that you will realize, understand, and discover the season you are in currently, embrace it, and actually celebrate it!

The Pear Tree

The following is a great parable that helps us understand seasons.

> *Once there was a man who had four sons. He wanted them to learn about life so he sent them each on a quest to go look at a pear tree that was a distance away.*

But he sent them each during a different season.

The first son went during winter. The second in spring. The third, summer. The youngest, fall.

They all returned at the end of the fourth season and described to their father what they saw.

The first son saw an ugly, bent, twisted, and cold and barren tree.

The second son saw a tree covered with green buds and full of promise.

The third son saw a tree laden with blossoms and smelled sweet and beautiful and its form was graceful.

The fourth son disagreed with all of them. He saw a tree ripe with fruit, full of life and fulfillment.

The father explained they were all correct because they had each seen the tree only in one season. He told them not to judge by only one season. The essence of who they are comes by the measure of all the seasons of life:

- Stand fast in winter.
- See the promise of spring.
- Appreciate the beauty of summer.
- Enjoy and reap the fulfillment and harvest of fall.

Important words to remember:

- Don't let the pain of one season destroy the rest.
- Don't judge life by one difficult season.
- A season will only last just that long, a season.
- The Lord will lead us into another season.
- Life is full of seasons and they're all different.

Prayers for the Seasons

To gain wisdom, knowledge, and discernment.

> *"God, grant me the serenity to accept the things I cannot change, courage to change the things I can; and wisdom to know the difference."*
>
> —Reinhold Niebuhr

Identify the season

> *Lord, I pray right now I will have the discernment to identify the season I am in currently. I will be able to recognize that season with all its pluses and minuses.*

Acceptance

> *Oh God, I pray for You to help me accept this season I am in. Even though I may be struggling, I need to realize You have me in this season for a reason and I'm willing to embrace it with all its prickly thorns as well as its fragrant floral aromas!*

Learn

Father in Heaven, let me learn what You have for me to learn. May I not just pray, Lord, deliver me from this season. But let me be a quick learner. Let Your grace carry me through. May I realize the good, bad, and ugly of each season. May I know Your will for my life through this particular season and learn all I can!

Grow

Lord Jesus, let me grow in wisdom and stature and in favor with You and people around me through this season. I want to be like You, Jesus. May I move farther down the road in this spiritual journey You have me on. I may hit bumps in the road, but I will have grown closer to You!

4

WINTER

Season of Breakthroughs

A spiritual winter season can be described as the coldness and harshness of life when we are facing:

- Struggles
- Depression
- Tough times

I remember the long, dark, cold winters of Canada. Sometimes the snow would almost cover our first-story windows. We couldn't see outside. We couldn't get outside because it was as high our garage door. Often schools wouldn't allow children to play outside for fear of frostbite. If cold enough, skin could freeze in 30 minutes, so recess would be held inside.

**REMEMBER:
TOUGH TIMES
DON'T LAST,
TOUGH PEOPLE DO!**

When experiencing a spiritual winter, it's important to realize that this season will end. Spring will break forth. Believe God is going to break through the tough circumstances of your life and work everything for your good.

As mentioned previously, our daughter experienced a terrible marriage and divorce. She went through months of counseling to recover from domestic abuse. At the time, it seemed there was nothing positive to hold on to. But when she came out on the other side, she saw God's hand of protection and provision. She was granted a university scholarship and was given the chance to return to school to change her life.

What's the issue stopping you from seeing the breakthrough? If you're hurting, discouraged, depressed, or abandoned, don't just freeze. Don't stand still and succumb to the frostbite. Press on.

The Breakthrough Story in Mark 2:1-8

A great breakthrough story is found in Mark 2:1-8. It's the story of the four men who bring their lame friend to Jesus for healing. He needed a breakthrough. He'd suffered in a winter season too long!

> *A few days later, when Jesus again entered Capernaum, the people heard that he had*

come home. They gathered in such large numbers that there was no room left, not even outside the door, and he preached the word to them. Some men came, bringing to him a paralyzed man, carried by four of them. Since they could not get him to Jesus because of the crowd, they made an opening in the roof above Jesus by digging through it and then lowered the mat the man was lying on. When Jesus saw their faith, he said to the paralyzed man, "Son, your sins are forgiven." Now some teachers of the law were sitting there, thinking to themselves, "Why does this fellow talk like that? He's blaspheming! Who can forgive sins but God alone?" Immediately Jesus knew in his spirit that this was what they were thinking in their hearts, and he said to them, "Why are you thinking these things?

There are *five keys* in this story that give us insights into breaking through our winter season.

1. The first key is making room for Jesus (see Mark 2:1-2). The house is crowded and there is no room for anyone else to fit into the space to receive a breakthrough. Life gets crowded. There's no room for anything else. My father used to say, "People will ultimately do what they want to do." If it's important to you—you'll make room. You'll force it.

My father passed away at the young age of 59. Four months later we dedicated our new church facility for the Free Methodist Church in London, Ontario. Two months after that, I was burned out and exhausted. The next month my mother called and invited us to visit her in Niagara Falls, a two-hour drive from London. I didn't want to go, I was wiped out. Then I saw I had penciled in on my calendar a conference being held in Niagara Falls, New York, and thought, *I need something. I need to be refreshed.*

We went to visit my mom and also attended the conference. There was something different about that conference. There was a woman preacher that night—Marilyn Hickey. She spoke words of life I had never heard before. The words lifted my spirit, picked me up. She encouraged everyone to return Saturday night for the anointing service. I wanted to attend, but it meant driving back from London and returning home late Saturday night.

Deborah and I knew we needed something and were determined to attend the anointing service. That Saturday morning everything went wrong. A church member was taken to the hospital with a heart attack. Our daughter, Elizabeth, was sick. Our car overheated. It was horrible. And we almost didn't go. But we were determined to go—so we made room. We pushed the clutter of obstacles out of our lives and went!

2. The second key is overcoming your paralysis (Mark 2:3). The crippled man did not have a defeatist mentality. He didn't just accept his circumstances. He was willing to overcome his winter season—his paralysis! Some of us are "paralyzed" by a

condemning past, chronic fears, and habitual sins. We need to pick ourselves up and make our way to the Lord of our breakthroughs!

What is the definition of insanity? Doing the same thing and expecting different results. God takes us through different seasons to bring new experiences into our lives. Sitting paralyzed in a state of lethargy is horribly self-defeating.

Statistics reveal that the average teenager spends more than nine hours a day on their smart phones. Wow! Now that's paralysis. Now that's a lethargy that imprisons and limits you from becoming productive and progressing in life.

Sometimes I want to scream in a restaurant, "Put your phones down and talk to each other!" Many have lost the art of connecting. We need to get out of our paralyzed stupor and start connecting with God, with each other, and even with ourselves.

3. The third key is being in the right company. The paralyzed man was surrounded with friends who were

willing to help him do whatever it took to get into that room where Jesus could heal him. They were willing to put their friend in a position to receive. Too many times we surround ourselves with naysayers who don't believe we can break through the harshness of the winter season. There's a saying, "Show me your friends and I'll show you your future."

When my kids would ask me, "How do I get friends?" I would tell them, "You need to be a friend to get a friend." What are you doing to invest in someone's life? It takes effort. When our oldest daughter was becoming a teenager, Deborah and I looked for a new home with a bit more space, and a pool. Even though the swimming season in Canada was short, I wanted our home to be a place where all our children's friends wanted to visit. Who are your friends? Who are you influencing? And who is influencing you?

4. The fourth key is refusing to be denied (see Mark 2:4). When the house

was full and overrun the friends with the paralyzed man did not turn back. Even though it wasn't convenient, even though it wasn't easy, they hauled their friend and his bed to the roof. They refused to be denied. In the harshness of winter, they refused to be frozen out! They pursued! They endured! They didn't give up!

5. The fifth key is to remove the lid of human limitation (Mark 2:4). The clay of the roof represents the humanity and limitation of the situation. The roof represents the limitation. We talk about glass ceilings. We talk about hitting the roof and not being able to go any higher. These five men removed human limitation in reaching out to Jesus.

If you want to finish your winter season and receive your breakthrough, you need to remove the lid of human limitation—of self-doubt and lack of self-esteem. A great example of this is Gideon, who said he was the least of his tribe (see Judges 6:15). Another example is Moses who insisted he wasn't the one because he stuttered (see Exodus 4:10). Human limitations—real or self-imposed—can be overcome. Our God specializes in bringing breakthrough supernaturally.

Spiritual Breakthrough

If you have had spiritual dryness during winter seasons, God is ready to break through! Remember, He has always been ready and willing to bring you victory! He stands at the door. He is always there ready to be invited into your life and give you a spiritual refreshing.

Satan is the one who says you are not worthy. He is a liar, and the father of lies! (See John 8:44.) He will do anything to keep you from enjoying the great things of God! Turn away from him and turn always toward Jesus who stands at your door knocking (see Revelation 3:20). You just need to open the door.

PRAYERS FOR THE WINTER SEASON

Admit How Hard it Is

Heavenly Father, I pray in this winter season, admitting how hard and difficult it is. I am struggling and need Your help to get through this difficult time. I can't make it without You and need You now more than ever! And actually, I admit that without You, Lord, I don't think I'm going to make it.

Cold and Unfeeling

It's hard to even confess this, Father God, but I'm feeling cold and unfeeling. I'm actually numb to emotions because I've been hurting so badly. I need You, O Lord, to understand this empty feeling I'm having.

Honest and Transparent

I'm willing to lay it all out before You, God. I'm going to be honest and transparent in all my emotions, or lack thereof. I want you to know, Lord, I have nothing left and nothing to hide. I need You right now, and every moment of every day!

Complaining

This is a little bit like Jeremiah's complaint. Where I am truly complaining to You, my heavenly Father. I know this is a struggle and You see me. But I wonder how long I will remain in this cold and barren land.

Strength and Peace

Lord, I specifically pray in this winter season for strength and peace. I need both of those now more than ever. Without Your strength and peace I won't make it. So please, God, supernaturally endue me with Your power and fill me with Your peace!

Ideas

What I need are God ideas, Jesus. In order to get through this season, I need God ideas. Something that goes beyond my understanding. Something that takes me beyond what I would normally think of. Let my mind land on some godly wild and crazy ideas that will get me through and out of this winter season. Thank You, Lord.

Friends

I need a friend right now. I feel all alone. I can't do this on my own. Please, Father, send into my life some God-given friends who will walk this journey with me. I don't necessarily need them to do something for me, just a commitment saying they are standing with me through it all!

Peace

Dear Jesus, thank You for the peace I feel deep down in my spirit that I know You have placed there through the Holy Spirit living in me. I will rest in that peace until this season has passed and I welcome the next season you have designed for me. Thank You.

5

SPRING

Season of Sowing and Reaping of Souls

Spring is a great season. I remember in Canada when the ice and hard-crusted snow would finally melt and suddenly the grass could be seen peeking out. The sight of the grass was inspirational and encouraging. It was time to buy seeds and get the lawn mower tuned up.

Spring is a time for planting—in the soil of the earth and the soil of our souls. Let's journey through the process together as we prepare the soil and plant good seeds in good soil.

> *Listen then to what the parable of the sower means: When anyone hears the message about the kingdom and does not understand it, the evil one comes and snatches away what was sown in their heart. This is the seed sown along the path. The seed falling on rocky ground refers to someone who hears the word and at once receives it with joy. But since they have no root, they last only a short time. When trouble or persecution comes because of the word, they quickly fall away. The seed falling among the thorns refers to someone who hears the word, but the worries of this life and the deceitfulness of wealth choke the word, making it unfruitful. But the seed falling on good soil refers to someone who hears the word and understands it. This is the one who*

produces a crop, yielding a hundred, sixty or thirty times what was sown (Matthew 13:18-23).

Prepare the Soil

Before we moved to Florida, I loved the season when the garden centers would open. Traditionally they opened on the May 24th holiday weekend. In the U.S., that's Memorial Day weekend. But in Canada, we celebrated it as Queen Victoria's birthday. The line-up at the cash registers would be long with people buying mulch, fertilizer, and flats of flowers and plants. Planting in Ontario couldn't begin before that date due to the danger of frost.

I loved our first year in Florida. It was February and I needed some things for house repairs from Home Depot. When I arrived, I saw the Garden Center bursting with plants and flowers and loads of mulch and fertilizer bags. I asked at the checkout what was going on. The clerk said, "The start of our gardening season in Florida is Valentine's Day!" Wow! I loved it!

I love getting things ready for planting. The debris of winter is gone and it's a fresh new adventure.

I remember my first church, Caistor Center, in Ontario, Canada. Everyone had a big garden. I'm not talking about flower gardens. They planted BIG vegetable gardens.

I tried to prepare a quarter-acre to start my own garden. The ground was hard, dark clay. But before I could plant the vegetable seeds, the ground really had to be worked over. I couldn't do it alone. I had to buy a rototiller. Without soil preparation, the seeds wouldn't germinate.

Use Good Seed

When living in Canada, each winter I looked forward to receiving seed catalogues in the mail and carefully picking out seeds and planning what to plant where. I quickly learned the value of good seeds. The discount dollar store offered them at a fantastic price, but when I planted them, I reaped a discount harvest. The more expensive seeds that had been pre-tested and evaluated cost much, much more. But the better the seed, the better the harvest. The bounty was more than double.

Plant in Good Soil

There are all types of ground and seeds fall on all types of ground. In Matthew 13 we read the story of the parable of the sower of seed. A farmer sows the seed, scattering it. It scatters in different places, on different soil. Matthew says the seed—the message about the Kingdom of God—falls on top of the path and the birds come and eat it. When it falls and is scorched by the sun, it withers. The shallow soil doesn't allow root growth. If the seed is placed among thorns, it's easily choked out and dies. But if the soil is fertile and has been prepared, its harvest is 30, 60, even 100-fold. Wow! What a great story!

Matthew tells us in verses 18-23 the application of the story. The path is the trampled-down soil. The soil is hardened, people hear the Good News but don't understand. If they don't understand, then *"the evil one comes and snatches away what was sown in their heart. This is the seed sown along the path."*

In the spring of a new Christian's life, the soil is easily packed down hard. The seed can't develop roots. The new Christian has received salvation and joy, but when trouble or persecution comes, it's easy to fall away and lose faith.

Jesus explains in this parable that if the soil isn't prepared, there will be no harvest—no fruit of the Spirit or spiritual victory.

Continue to believe for those you've been praying. If they've heard the Word, then they're ready for some seed. At first, for some, their hearts are hardened, like the pathway. They are trampled down and the seed has a hard time breaking through. Pray for them to be rototilled. When they're tender to the things of God, the Word falls on good soil. When the time is right, growth can begin. People hardened to the pain of life can't feel the joy of the Gospel until their hearts are prepared.

Rocky Place

Seeds sown on the rocky place—these people receive joy, but no root is established. The Good News seeds sown lasts only for a short time. The soil is usually receptive, unless there are stones in the way that keep our hearts from getting down into the good soil. Rocks of life cover up the good things and take over. What rock is in your way? Business? Financial fears? Adultery? These rocks keep the seed from reaching the soil so it can establish good roots. So, when trouble and difficulties come, there aren't enough roots to keep the seedling intact and growing. It dies off.

Thorns

Sometimes thorns sprout up with the seedlings. Sometimes the difference is hard to distinguish between the two. Without warning, the weeds in life spring up and overgrow what's meant to be good. In the beginning, you can't really tell they are thorns. They appear to be seedlings from the seed of the Word. But all of a sudden, there is this thorny weed right beside you.

The weeds in life come to take you out! Jesus says weeds become the worries of life and the deceitfulness of wealth. No one can sustain life on weeds. Take this to heart and be careful not to allow weeds to invade your garden of God's good Word to feed your soul.

When praying for others, be aware of the different soil your seed falls upon. Sometimes it seems the loved ones we are trying to win for the Lord have hearts full of all these soil types. The pathway is a hardened heart. The rocks are indicative of shallow soil. The thorns grow up alongside, choking out the Kingdom's plantings.

Prepare the soil, get good seed, and cast it again and again and again. It may seem redundant and repetitive. But I believe that's what works.

Then once you've cast the seed. Leave it alone. Don't go poking at it, stirring things up. After a farmer plants seed, he doesn't dig around in the soil seeing if growth has taken place. He lets nature take its course. The seed has power to grow on its own. Plant it, and the soil has power to bring the seed to life. Leave it alone!

Trust that the seed of the Gospel has the power of life within it, that when it falls into the fertile soil of someone's heart the seed will come to life and bring forth fruit of faith and salvation.

Jesus told them another parable: "The kingdom of heaven is like a man who sowed good seed in his field. But while everyone was sleeping, his enemy came and sowed weeds among the wheat, and went away. When the wheat sprouted and formed heads, then the weeds also appeared.

"The owner's servants came to him and said, 'Sir, didn't you sow good seed in your field? Where then did the weeds come from?'

"'An enemy did this,' he replied.

"The servants asked him, 'Do you want us to go and pull them up?'

"'No,' he answered, 'because while you are pulling the weeds, you may uproot the wheat with them. Let both grow together until the harvest. At that time I will tell the harvesters: First collect the weeds and tie them in bundles to be burned; then gather the wheat and bring it into my barn'" (Matthew 13:24-30).

In Matthew 13:24-30, Jesus specifically says the enemy plants the weeds. But when He is asked about pulling them up, Jesus says to leave them alone. We need to be assured God has everything under His control. He is the One who will take care of separating the harvest.

THE SEED OF THE GOSPEL HAS LIFE-GIVING POWER TO OVERCOME THE ENEMY.

There is one thing you can do, though—pray for rain! The rain of the Holy Spirit falls from Heaven onto the seed and brings it to life. For the farmer, if there isn't rain, it doesn't matter how good the seed or soil is, it won't grow. The seed must have the life-giving power of rain.

The seed of the Gospel has that same life-giving power. For that seed to come to life, we need the rain of the Holy Spirit to cause it to germinate and live.

Summary

To sow and reap souls for the Kingdom, we need four important ingredients for a good harvest:

- Good seed
- Good soil
- Rain
- MiracleGro

MiracleGro? Another crucial aspect of sowing and reaping is faith—we must believe it will grow. I like to call this MiracleGro!

Stand on Proverbs 22:6: *"Start children off on the way they should go, and even when they are old they will not turn from it."* Realize your children know your heart. If you've raised them in a Christian home, took them to church, prayed for them, and sowed good seed into them, they know. They know your heart. They know where you stand. They know what you've done and have invested in them. Have you been perfect? No, of course not. But God knows as well. He knows your heart, not just your deeds. He still loves you.

GOD KNOWS YOUR HEART AND LOVES YOU.

I shared previously about our daughter, Emily, and the prayers I said over her when she was lost and wandering away. Every time I spoke to her or sent her a text it would include these three phrases: "I love you, I care about you, I'm praying for you." I had this picture in my spirit that she was drowning out in the sea, and I was on the ship throwing a life preserver to her. Praying that one of the times I threw it to her, she'd grab hold and I'd pull her out of the waters she was drowning in. Catch it—I love you—grab it—I care about you—hold on—I'm praying for you!

The last verse in preparing for a harvest is found in Hebrews 11:1: *"Now faith is confidence in what we hope for and assurance about what we do not see."* When you put that seed into the ground, you have to believe it's going to bear fruit. You have to have *faith* there is power in that seed. You have to have faith the soil of our loved ones' souls will bring forth faith. You have to believe the rain of the Holy Spirit will work in that seed. Faith is being sure they will come home!

> *Jesus continued: "There was a man who had two sons. The younger one said to his father, 'Father, give me my share of the estate.' So he divided his property between them.*
>
> *"Not long after that, the younger son got together all he had, set off for a distant country and there squandered his wealth in wild living. After he had spent everything, there was a severe famine in that whole country, and he began to be in need. So he went and hired himself out to a citizen of that country, who sent him to his fields to feed pigs. He longed to fill his stomach with the pods that the pigs were eating, but no one gave him anything.*

"When he came to his senses, he said, 'How many of my father's hired servants have food to spare, and here I am starving to death! I will set out and go back to my father and say to him: Father, I have sinned against heaven and against you. I am no longer worthy to be called your son; make me like one of your hired servants.' So he got up and went to his father.

"But while he was still a long way off, his father saw him and was filled with compassion for him; he ran to his son, threw his arms around him and kissed him.

The son said to him, 'Father, I have sinned against heaven and against you. I am no longer worthy to be called your son.'

"But the father said to his servants, 'Quick! Bring the best robe and put it on him. Put a ring on his finger and sandals on his feet. Bring the fattened calf and kill it. Let's have a feast and celebrate. For this son of mine was dead and is alive

again; he was lost and is found.' So they began to celebrate.

"Meanwhile, the older son was in the field. When he came near the house, he heard music and dancing. So he called one of the servants and asked him what was going on. 'Your brother has come,' he replied, 'and your father has killed the fattened calf because he has him back safe and sound.'

"The older brother became angry and refused to go in. So his father went out and pleaded with him. But he answered his father, 'Look! All these years I've been slaving for you and never disobeyed your orders. Yet you never gave me even a young goat so I could celebrate with my friends. But when this son of yours who has squandered your property with prostitutes comes home, you kill the fattened calf for him!'

"'My son,' the father said, 'you are always with me, and everything I have is yours.

But we had to celebrate and be glad, because this brother of yours was dead and is alive again; he was lost and is found'" (Luke 15:11-32).

My favorite verse for preparing for a season of sowing and reaping souls is the story of the prodigal son found in Luke 15:11-32. The son drifts a long way from his family. He's lost to them. But as the father believes he will come home, verse 17 says that the son came to his senses. I believe there is a point when our lost children will come to their senses. It says in verse 20 that the son started to make his journey home. And while he was still a long way off, the father had faith to wait until he saw him coming down the pathway. Even when our children are a long way off we can be waiting for them to come home. We can have faith to wait to see them coming down the pathway, and walking back into our lives through the open door of our hearts.

See now in your spirit that even though your wayward child or loved one maybe a long way off, they will come to their senses and come home! Look ahead and visualize them walking home, back into your life through the open door of your heart. Your lost child or loved one will come back to their senses and come home to you and to God.

Again, remember and believe Hebrews 11:1 (NKJV), *"Now faith is the substance of things hoped for, the evidence of things not seen."*

Conclusion

Jesus says in John 12:24: "*...unless a kernel of wheat [a seed] falls to the ground and dies, it remains only a single seed. But if it dies, it produces many seeds.*" There is life in the seed. However, it doesn't come to life until it's gone through a death process. I don't know why it hurts so much, but planting the seeds for wayward children is hard. Shallow ground is painful.

It's especially hard for parents to go through the seed-death process with our children. I speak from experience, as our youngest daughter was a prodigal. It was hard. But her mother and I kept believing. It was hard to watch her make poor choices. It was heartbreaking to watch the thorns grow and choke her life.

In the Spirit, the seeds were cast on the soil of her soul. They took root, and began to spring to life. Finally, she began to make her way back home and back to God. It took more time than we desired, but the seeds matured. Amazing opportunities have come into place for her as a believer. I'm a believer too in the spring season of sowing and reaping of souls!

Prayers for the Spring Season

Who in Your Life?

Lord, right now I am burdened for_________. I have been sowing seeds into them. I'm believing for a harvest of that seed in their life. That they will respond and reach out to You and all that You have for them. And Lord, as I sow that seed, I'm going to leave and let go into the ground, believing that it will spring forth life.

Preparing the Soil

Heavenly Father, help me to understand what it is to prepare good soil. To till the hardened soil. To realize that You will help me with getting the soil ready for the seed of Your word into their hearts so it will bring forth a harvest of faith!

Good Seed

Jesus, help me to see what good seed is, and where it is. That I will be able to plant good seed to bring forth a great harvest. I thank You now for the seed that has grown in my life, and I can now propagate and plant good seed.

Type of Soil

As I get ready to plant good seed for a harvest, Lord, give me discernment to see what type of soil I am planting it in. That it isn't hardened, thorny, or shallow soil. I want the seed to be planted into soil that will bear fruit 100, 200 and 1,000-fold!

Faith for the Seed

And now, Lord, as I plant the seed, let me have faith that it will fall into the ground, die, and then live and sprout. Help me to have patience to not go poking around at the seed to see if it's ready to sprout. Let me trust You and have faith in the way You created all things to bear fruit of itself.

Bearing Fruit

And God, I pray that the seed I've planted will have success in bringing forth a wonderful harvest. That it will truly bring forth a bountiful harvest! I am believing for this harvest. And I will praise You for that bounty!

6

SUMMER

Season of Miracles

The summer season is a season of miracles. In the summer we see the fullness of everything! Crops are growing. Leaves and flowers are in bloom. The winter is gone and the sun is warm. In the summer, it seems like all of nature is operating in an innate power! The days are rich and full of new life!

Jesus says in John 14:12, that we will be doing *"greater things."* What is greater than what Jesus did during His three years of earthly ministry? He raised the dead, and He brought sight to the blind. Yet greater things happen when we walk in the fullness of the Holy Spirit. Miracles occur beyond our understanding and our expectations. We need to open our minds and hearts to *"greater things."*

How is greater defined? Think beyond the normal expectation. The miracle of seeing a seed going into the ground and sprouting a plant is one thing, but seeing it bear fruit with hundreds of other life-bearing seeds is another. That is amazing! After the seed is planted it bears fruit. That's the norm. When it bears 100 times—that is amazing. That is greater, a miracle.

The summer season of life reaps miracles beyond expectation.

When the founders of New York City laid out the plan for development, they began in the center and numbered the streets outward. Only six or seven streets existed at the time. Thinking in long-range terms, they projected a possible 19 streets.

They called 19th street, Boundary Street, because surely New York City could never become larger! But even with their broadmindedness, history has proven them shortsighted. At last count, the city has reached 284th street. Their expectations were too limited.

We need to let the summer season blossom in our lives with miracles that far exceed our expectations. God's desire is for you to walk in the fullness of His Spirit.

> *But the fruit of the Spirit is love, joy, peace, forbearance, kindness, goodness, faithfulness, gentleness and self-control. Against such things there is no law* (Galatians 5:22-23).

In the summer season of life, look for fruit that's ready to be picked. Paul tells us in Galatians 5:22-23 to look for characteristics of that spiritual fruit. Notice that the *fruit* of the Spirit is singular, not plural. There are nine characteristics of that fruit: love, joy, peace, patience, kindness, goodness, faithfulness, gentleness, and self-control.

Just before this list (Galatians 5:20-21), is listed the sins of the flesh. What Paul is saying, get rid of the sins of the flesh so you have room for the fruit of the Spirit to grow.

Your Spiritual Gifts

When the sins of the flesh are gone, the fruit can grow bigger and better. As the fruit grows, and you get rid of the sins of the flesh, you are able to walk in your gifts. The best way for you to see the fullness of summer is to serve in your spiritual gifts. If God has called you to be a peach, you can't be an apple. You need to operate in your gifts.

How do you discover your spiritual gifts? One way is to read about them and perhaps take a spiritual gifts discovery test through your church, a ministry, or there are many good ones online that are free. Take several different tests and see what you learn. But don't stop there.

Once you discover what your spiritual gift or gifts are, you need to develop the gift. Try teaching or preaching in a small setting. If you receive confirmation, keep looking for opportunities to use the gift. God will provide them. If there's no confirmation or developing fruit, look for another gift. There's one for you. Don't give up.

I remember when my wife took a cake-decorating course. She had an icing pedestal that she twirled between her thumb and index finger. With her other hand, she piped icing on the pedestal to make the most beautiful rose. I sat and watched her, mesmerized how easy it looked. After she made several of these beautiful icing roses, I decided to try. As I took the pedestal in one hand and the tube of icing in the other, I just made a mess! I knew then that decorating cakes was *not* my gifting!

As a teenager, my first job was working in a restaurant. I realized I had a knack for cooking. Now, my wife and I make a great team; I make it taste good and she makes it look good. The first Wednesday of each month we have a potluck supper before our family night at church.

Suppose someone dropped their plate of desserts they had selected from the buffet table. This is how people with different gifts would respond:

- ***Gift of prophecy:*** "I knew that would happen."
- ***Gift of service:*** "Oh, let me help you clean it up."
- ***Gift of teaching:*** "The reason it fell was because it was too heavy on one side."
- ***Gift of exhortation:*** "Next time, maybe you should let someone else carry it."
- ***Gift of giving:*** "Here, you can have my dessert."
- ***Gift of mercy:*** "Don't feel too bad. It could happen to anyone."
- ***Gift of administration:*** "Jim, would you get the mop? Sue, please help pick this up. Mary, could you get him another dessert?"

We've all been gifted differently and so we act differently and we serve differently.

I truly believe that in each church there are all the gifts needed in order to function as an effective, biblical Christian community. *"Therefore you do not lack any spiritual gift as you eagerly wait for our Lord Jesus Christ to be revealed"* (1 Corinthians 1:7). This verse was written to the entire church at Corinth. Even with all its problems, this community of faith did not lack any spiritual gift.

After the fruit has grown, during the summer season we will look for the will of God. We now see the summer season is a season of the fullness of God, so we grow the fruit of God, and receive and use God's will for our lives.

Yes, He does have a will, plan, and purpose for you. I believe that when you allow His will to be fulfilled in your life, it will be accomplished in ways you cannot imagine or even dream or think about!

His Divine Will

One of the main questions being asked by believers is how do we discover His divine will? First, let's not just move forward saying, "Lord, bless all I do." Let's ask what He wants us to do before we act. First, submit to His will, plan, and purpose for your life.

Before you go a step farther, tell the Lord you will do whatever He asks. Second, take it one step at a time. If you're anything like me, you want to know the end from the beginning. But as I've journeyed with the Lord in ministry for almost 40 years, I have come to realize that life with the Lord is a journey, not just a destination. The outcome is always different from what I could've imagined. It's a *faith* walk! Take one step at a time.

SUBMIT TO HIS WILL, PLAN, AND PURPOSE FOR YOUR LIFE—AND TAKE ONE STEP AT A TIME.

Where do you fit in the Body of Christ? In thinking of a physical body, every part fits perfectly, and every part is important, so too with the Body of Christ. If the Lord has called you to be a kneecap in the body, you can't decide to become an elbow. It just won't fit. Ever bang your elbow and hurt your funny bone? It isn't funny! But after that hurt, you don't all of a sudden say, "I no longer want to have an elbow, because it hurts sometimes." No, you have two elbows that work in tandem with your arms to assist your whole body to function properly. Likewise, your spiritual gift, or gifts, won't and can't fit somewhere other than where God placed you to use it in the Body of Christ.

Too often in the church people get offended and say, "I no longer want to be part of the Body of Christ here, I'm going to change and connect elsewhere." I don't see that working for the good of the Body. Too many people in our organized churches today have a revolving door mentality where they move and transfer from place to place, hoping their elbow can become a knee cap someplace else.

Seeing God do something great in your life is believing it can be done! Since the days of the ancient Greeks there were efforts for runners to break the four-minute mile. Some found old records of how the Greeks tried to accomplish this. For example, they had wild animals chase the runners, hoping that would make them run faster. They tried drinking tiger's milk—not the milk you get at the supermarket, I'm talking about the real thing. Nothing worked, so they decided it was physically impossible for a human being to run a mile in less than four minutes. They stated that our bone structure was all wrong, the wind resistance was too great, and our lung power was inadequate. There were many reasons.

Then one day, one human being proved that the doctors, the trainers, and the athletes themselves were all wrong. And, miracle of miracles, in 1954 Roger Bannister broke the four-minute mile. And the year after that, 300 runners broke the four-minute mile! It only takes one.

It only takes one person to believe in the possibility and make it a reality.

Believe God can and will do the exceptional for you.

Believe God can and will do the exceptional for you. Put your life and spiritual gifts in His hands and become exceptional.

Always Hope

I studied revivals as part of my academic doctoral work. Historically, churches don't survive long, protracted revivals. So, coming to Brownsville Assembly, the place of the longest and largest revival in U.S. history, was a risk in that it presented many challenges. When I arrived, the church was struggling. It was in desperate straits—numerically, spiritually, and financially. And here we are now, more than 15 years later, still here and thriving! I believed that Brownsville would prove history wrong and come back as a mighty church.

After coming to Brownsville Assembly, I discovered that Brownsville was a community—one of the most impoverished, struggling neighborhoods in the Florida panhandle. Officials told me that from Mobile, Alabama, to Jacksonville, Florida, the Brownsville community was at the top of every negative statistic.

The 32505 zip code was top of the list for crime, violent crime, domestic violence, prostitution, drug arrests, truancy, juvenile delinquency, and poverty. And so the story went that the Brownsville community was horrible and hopeless. One official said, "Brownsville Community is hopeless and there's no point in pouring any more money down that rat hole!"

But again, I believe nothing is hopeless with the power of God. We are in the process of revitalizing the Brownsville neighborhood with a grocery store, restaurant, bank, community center, and an affordable senior-housing project.

But that story is for another book! I do believe the community of Brownsville will continue to see another summer season.

Sweet-Smelling Fruit

Realize that God uses the negative experiences in life as fertilizer. When we push through them, the fruit in our life becomes bigger and better as a result.

I always remember the delight of driving through the fruit belt of Ontario. No one enjoys the smell of fertilizer, but when the fruit blossoms appear, the beautiful aroma is a pleasure. In the fall, the bounty is displayed on quaint country road stands and shipped all around the world for nutrition and enjoyment. That's what God does in and through us. He has the ability to make something beautiful in our lives. He brings sweet fruit to our personal ministry and our mission.

As I traveled through the Niagara Fruit Belt in Ontario, Canada, and now the orange groves of Florida, I see how the crops are cultivated. I remember driving by an orange juice plant and enjoying the aroma of the oranges being made into juice.

I see the fruit stands along the roads and the baskets and bushels full of peaches and apples. I realize God has put within His creation the ability to bring sweetness in our lives with a fullness of ministry and mission.

Questions to Consider

The following are a few questions to consider during your summer season:

- Are you seeking God's fullness in your life?
- Are you bearing the fruit of the Spirit?
- Are you walking and using your gifting(s)?
- Are you submitted to God's will in your life?
- Have you actually taken the first steps to see His will accomplished in your life?
- Do you know where you fit in the Body of Christ?

Prayers for the Fullness of God

Expecting Fullness

Lord, now that I have planted, and now that I am seeing the beginning of the sprouting of the seeds, I am full of expectant faith. I am expecting a fullness for the seeds I have planted. I thank You for the fullness that is becoming evident in my life.

The Fruit of the Spirit

O God, as I am moving forward with fullness in my life, I thank You for growing the fruit of the Spirit in my life. I know it's hard to see fruit grow, but I can now see the beginnings of that fruit. I realize it's not different fruit, but one fruit with different characteristics.

Walking in the Fullness of His Gifts

As that fruit is growing, I realize I have gifts You've given me. I am more open to seeing those gifts come to pass in my life, and I am excited to see how You are going to use me next. I pray my eyes are open to seeing opportunities for those gifts to be used in my everyday life.

Submission to His will

I realize that in order for fruit to grow and gifts to be experienced, I need to live a submitted life. So, Lord, I surrender everything to You. In this season of fullness, I need to submit my journey to You!

Take the First Step

Lord, I pray right now that You will show me the first step I need to take to start walking in the fullness of this season. I ask You to clearly lay out what that first step is, and I commit and promise You I will do it!

My Fit in the Body of Christ

Lord Jesus, thank You for promising me in Your Word that I fit in the Body of Christ. That I belong. That I have a place. I thank You for that place. I thank You for the confirmation and assurance of where I fit. I thank You for giving me a church family, that part of the Body of Christ where I belong. And I promise to be part of that Body in that place so I won't be tempted to remove myself and try to attach myself somewhere else! I thank You, Lord, that I am unique and I fit in this Body and belong here.

7

FALL

Season of Provision and Blessing

I remember all too well my first pastorate. Deborah and I had been married three years. We had spent those first three years at Asbury Seminary in Kentucky in the U.S. We had graduated from Spring Arbor University in May, were married two weeks later, and moved that summer to Kentucky.

I distinctly remember that first Labor Day weekend at my first church. I had always gone to school the first day after Labor Day. Now for the first time in 20 years, instead of going to school, I walked across the field from the parsonage to the church, through the sanctuary and to the right of the platform and pulpit, and through the door to the pastor's study.

At that time, my salary was $150 a week. And I remember that the parsonage had a cistern for the water for the house. All the water from the roof would go down the eaves troughs and into the cistern in the basement. Every month or so, I'd throw in a cup of bleach to kill any bacteria. I'd take my little Ford Fiesta car and travel down the country roads visiting parishioners. Then came the first Thanksgiving.

The Women's Missionary Society (WMS) called me saying that each year the church would set up a harvest display at the front of the church. And they wanted to make sure I was okay with that. I thought, *How nice!* Most of the congregants had farms or at least large gardens. They want to bring their firstfruits to the church. In Canada, Thanksgiving is celebrated the second Monday in October; but this year we celebrated it on the fourth Thursday in November, as the U.S. commemorates the bountiful harvest meal shared between the Pilgrims and the Wampanoag Indians in 1621.

The week before Thanksgiving, the platform of that little church was filled with produce. They brought dozens of squash, bushels of apples and peaches, canned preserves, tomatoes, and pickles. The platform was full!

I thought, *How beautiful. What a glorious display of God's bounty!* After the service, I was standing at the rear door of the sanctuary greeting the congregation as they left and wishing them all a happy Thanksgiving. The president of the WMS said, "Pastor, you do know that the harvest display is all yours and Deborah's, right?" It meant so much. What a blessing. What a provision of God's goodness and bounty!

Deuteronomy 26 tell us about the children of Israel in the Promised Land. They are given guidelines of the land:

When you have entered the land the Lord your God is giving you as an inheritance and have taken possession of it and settled in it, take some of the firstfruits of all that you produce from the soil of the land the Lord your God is giving you and put them in a basket. Then go to the place the Lord your God will choose as a dwelling for his Name and say to the priest in office at the time, "I declare today to the Lord your God that I have come to the land the Lord swore to our ancestors to give us." The priest shall take the basket from your hands and set it down in front of the altar of the Lord your God. Then you shall declare before the Lord your God: "My father was a wandering Aramean, and he went down into Egypt with a few people and lived there and became a great nation, powerful and numerous. But the Egyptians mistreated us and made us suffer, subjecting us to harsh labor. Then we cried out to the Lord, the God of our ancestors, and the Lord heard our voice and saw our misery, toil and oppression. So the Lord brought us out of Egypt with a mighty hand and an outstretched arm, with great terror and with signs and wonders. He brought us to this place and gave us this land, a land flowing with milk and honey; and now I bring the firstfruits of the soil that you, Lord, have given me." Place the basket before the Lord your God and bow down before him. Then you and the Levites and the foreigners residing among you shall rejoice in all the good things the Lord your God has given to you and your household.

When you have finished setting aside a tenth of all your produce in the third year, the year of the tithe, you shall give it to the Levite, the foreigner, the fatherless and the widow, so that they may eat in your towns and be satisfied. Then say to the Lord your God: "I have removed from my house the sacred portion and have given it to the Levite, the foreigner, the fatherless and the widow, according to all you commanded. I have not turned aside from your commands nor have I forgotten any of them. I have not eaten any of the sacred portion while I was in mourning, nor have I removed any of it while I was unclean, nor have I offered any of it to the dead. I have obeyed the Lord my God; I have done everything you commanded me. Look down from heaven, your holy dwelling place, and bless your people Israel and the land you have given us as you promised on oath to our ancestors, a land flowing with milk and honey."

The Lord your God commands you this day to follow these decrees and laws; carefully observe them with all your heart and with all your soul. You have declared this day that the Lord is your God and that you will walk in obedience to him, that you will keep his decrees, commands and laws—that you will listen to him. And the Lord has declared this day that you

> *are his people, his treasured possession as he promised, and that you are to keep all his commands. He has declared that he will set you in praise, fame and honor high above all the nations he has made and that you will be a people holy to the Lord your God, as he promised.*

The fall season is a season of giving thanks for our firstfruits. We certainly need to be thankful for the small things. I think we take for granted so many of the small things that God has blessed us with. God has provided us so much. The United States of America is the greatest nation on earth; even with all our problems, it's still a great nation. We must give thanks to God for our jobs, homes, and families. Give thanks for the fire department and garbage collection. Give thanks for free speech and for freedom.

Right now as you read this, stop for a moment. Close your eyes. Take a breath. Hold it. Listen to your heart beating. Let out your breath. Open your eyes. Now be thankful your heart is working, your lungs are working, and your eyes are working.

Be thankful for the little things—they are great blessings indeed.

We need be thankful for the harvest we did not sow. When we go to the grocery store, we expect there to be bread, fruit, and vegetables. We didn't do anything to sow them, to tend the field, or to harvest them. Be thankful for God's promises! And for those who use their God-given gifts and talents to provide provision.

John 4:37-38 states, *"Thus the saying, 'One sows and another reaps' is true. I sent you to reap what you have not worked for. Others have done the hard work, and you have reaped the benefits of their labor."*

When I enter the sanctuary of Brownsville church, I sense God's presence in that building. From the first time I set foot in that place, His presence was there! I haven't done anything to deserve His presence, but He is there!

We all need to be thankful for the promise of provision. I love the fact that Jesus during His earthly ministry promised to provide for us. Jesus told us specifically not to worry:

"Therefore I tell you, do not worry about your life, what you will eat or drink; or about your body, what you will wear. Is not life more than food, and the body more than clothes? Look at the birds of the air; they do not sow or reap or store away in barns, and yet your heavenly Father feeds them. Are you not much more valuable than they? Can any one of you by worrying add a single hour to your life?

"And why do you worry about clothes? See how the flowers of the field grow. They do not labor or spin. Yet I tell you that not even Solomon in all his splendor was dressed like one of these. If that is how God clothes the grass of the field, which is here today and tomorrow is thrown into the fire, will he not much more clothe you—you of little faith? So do not worry, saying, 'What shall we eat?' or 'What shall we drink?' or 'What shall we wear?'" (Matthew 6:25-31).

I have been an adjunct faculty member with Global University for many years. One of my favorite courses is Synoptic Gospels. It's the study of the first three books of the New Testament.

In Matthew, Mark, and Luke, there are the two aspects of Jesus' ministry that are shared over and over—His parables and His miracles. They go hand in hand. The parables are life stories that illustrate life principles.

The miracles are a demonstration of His power in our lives to provide for our needs. The parables convey some pretty strong precepts in understanding God and His care for us. His miracles demonstrate He cares by doing! It's great to know our God is not just a God of words, but demonstration, action, and power.

Jesus didn't just *say* He'll provide for us and we need not worry. He takes action to back up His promise and admonition. When the crowd of 5000 was hungry, He fed them with five loaves of bread and two fish. How did He do that? It was the miracle of provision.

As I'm writing this right now, there is a need in the church for a miracle of provision. And I am believing for it! I pray by the time this book is published, I will have to add to this chapter about the practical miracle of provision. What am I thankful for?

- I am thankful He will provide!
- I am thankful for firstfruits!
- I am thankful for small things!
- I am thankful for reaping what I haven't sown!
- I am thankful for the promise God will provide!

Conclusion

Fall is a beautiful season. As I mentioned, in Canada, Thanksgiving is the second Monday of October. My birthday is October 10, and quite often my birthday falls on Thanksgiving weekend. And sometimes my birthday is actually on the

Monday of Thanksgiving. The fall colors are about at their peak during that week.

I distinctly remember one year as a child, I believe I was in the fourth grade, I had a *Globe and Mail* paper route. The newspapers had to be delivered by 7:00 in the morning. I would get up at 5:30 A.M. and start delivery by 6:0097 A.M.

It was Monday of Thanksgiving that year, October 10, my birthday. I got up early and delivered the papers. I returned home about 7:10 and my mother met me at the door. She was feeling sorry for me that I had to go out and deliver papers so early on my birthday, on Thanksgiving Day. It was my tenth birthday. I said, "Mom, you don't need to worry about me." I told her it was beautiful out that morning, the leaves were perfect. It had rained slightly and the sun was hitting the rain still on the leaves and the colors of fall shone beautifully. I remember those fall seasons with great fondness.

The leaves change color in the fall because they are dying and falling away. It's God's way of saying sometimes even when things die off there is still beauty. Let the old pass away. Let God bring a new season into your life.

Second Corinthians 5:17 says, "*Therefore, if anyone is in Christ, the new creation has come. The old has gone, and the new is here!*"

Prayers for the Harvest

His Promise to Provide

Lord, my heart is full of gratitude for this season of harvest. I am thankful, O God, for the bounty that comes. It is a promise in Your Word that You will provide. I need not worry or be concerned that You won't provide, because You have and You will.

Thankful for First Fruits

I am thankful, Lord, for firstfruits. I realize that You have provided so much for me and I need to give You the firstfruits of my life. I understand, Lord, You will bless me with the harvest, and I commit to You now the firstfruits of that harvest. Whether that harvest is a paycheck, a blessing, or whatever, the firstfruits are Yours and I commit them to You!

Thankful for the Small Things

Lord, I pray for big things. But right now I want to stop and say thank You for the small things of life. I thank You that You bless me in so many ways that I take many of them for granted. But I want to say thank You for those small things—for my breath, for my sight, for the roof over my head, the clothes on my back, and the food I partake of daily. You have blessed me with so many small things—that are in reality so very great indeed.

Thankful for Reaping What I Have Not Sown

I realize when I shop at the grocery store, Lord, I buy food that I did not sow. Yes, I pay for it, but someone else planted, nurtured, and harvested for me. I am thankful for Your creation that provides oil to make gasoline for my vehicle to run, for food that I eat, and electricity that operates my lights, furnace, and appliances in my home.

CONCLUSION

I have outlined what I see as four different seasons of life. I can tell you from experience I have been through each of these four seasons, most several times! Sometimes I have felt a particular season would never end. I have also felt I've breezed through some seasons that I would've liked to last a bit longer. There is no earthly timing in determining the duration of spiritual seasons. Just as we say spring starts March 21 or fall commences

September 21, the weather may tell us something quite different from what the calendar states.

I have also found the seasons of life are not in sequential order either. You can certainly have a fall Harvest season, then go into a summer season, then skip spring and plunge right into winter. There is no strict order to the seasons of life.

I believe that is why it is vital to evaluate your life and ask the Lord what is the current season you are going through. Once you've determined what season you are in, it is almost as important to ascertain the right response to that season. *How can I embrace the current climate and what can or may I get out of it? What can I learn about God and myself during this time?*

In God's economy, He doesn't do anything by accident—He uses all of our experiences to His benefit and glory. We need to open our eyes and ears and learn all that He is trying to teach us.

I pray the Lord will continue to direct your path through the seasons of your life so you can determine, embrace, respond, and learn from every seasonal change that occurs.

ABOUT THE AUTHOR

Dr. Evon Horton has 40 years of ministry experience. He currently pastors Brownsville Assembly of God in Pensacola, Florida, home of the largest and longest revival in U.S. history. He loves the moving of the Holy Spirit. He has pastored in Toronto, Canada, and has been president of Master's College and Seminary in Ontario, Canada. He is a devoted husband and father, and loves spoiling his three grandchildren. He is a true Disney freak!